D1199246

REAL LIFE MATH

journey to
THE MOON

Wendy Clemson and David Clemson

Ticktock

This library edition published in 2014 by Ticktock
First published in the USA in 2013 by Ticktock,
an imprint of Octopus Publishing Group Ltd

Distributed by Black Rabbit Books
P.O. Box 3263, Mankato, MN 56002

Cataloging-in-Publication Data is available from the Library of Congress
ISBN 978 1 78325 187 2

Printed and bound in China

1 3 5 7 9 10 8 6 4 2

Picture credits
t=top, b=bottom, c=center, l-left, r=right, f=far
Christian Deforeit 15; ESA/J Huart 3FL, 6L; NASA 5, 8, 10, 16B, 16T, 17T, 22, 23, 24B, 24T, 25, 26, 29T, 29B;
Jerry Mason/Science Photo Library 19; Science Photo Library/NASA 17B, 27;
Detlev van Ravenswaay/Science Photo Library 20-21B; Shutterstock 1, 4 (all), 9B, 11, 12-13 (all), 31T, 31B;
TickTock archive 2, 3L, 3C, 3R, 3FR, 6-7, 9T, 20, 21TL, 21TR, 28, 30.
Cover images: all from TickTock archive except front cover main picture of astronaut from NASA.

Every effort has been made to trace the copyright holders, and we apologize in advance for any unintentional omissions.
We would be pleased to insert the appropriate acknowledgement in any subsequent edition of this publication.

Contents

MATH SKILLS COVERED
IN THIS BOOK:

Numbers and the number system
Odds and evens: pp. 6–7
Adding ten: pp. 8–9
Number line: pp. 12–13
Skip-counting by twos: pp. 18–19
Comparing numbers: pp. 20–21
Sharing: pp. 24–25
Number pairs: pp. 26–27

Shape, space, and measurements
Telling time: pp. 8–9, 10–11,
12–13, 16–17, 27
Solid shapes: pp. 10–11
Scales and dials: pp. 18–19
Putting measures in order: pp. 22–23
Measures: pp. 28–29

Organizing data
Calendar: pp. 22–23
Grid maps: pp. 24–25
Bar graph: pp. 26–27

Problem solving
Missing numbers: p. 12
Number sequences: p. 14
Capacity: p. 17
Mystery numbers: p. 19
Weight: p. 24

Mental calculations
Addition and subtraction: pp. 14–15

**Supports math
standards for
ages 8+**

Welcome to Space

You have an amazing job – you're an astronaut! You will be taking your first trip into space very soon. What will it be like? You think it will be fun to be weightless and float around in your rocket. You're also looking forward to seeing planet Earth out of the window. Let's go!

Lots of people want to be astronauts.
The people who are chosen have some special skills.

Astronauts are scientists and carry out important research.

Some astronauts are top pilots. They fly rockets and planes.

Anyone who goes into space must be very fit.

You're living in a tiny space, and so you must get on well with other people.

But did you know that astronauts have to use math?

In this book you will find lots of number puzzles that astronauts have to solve every day. You will also get the chance to answer lots of number questions about your space adventure.

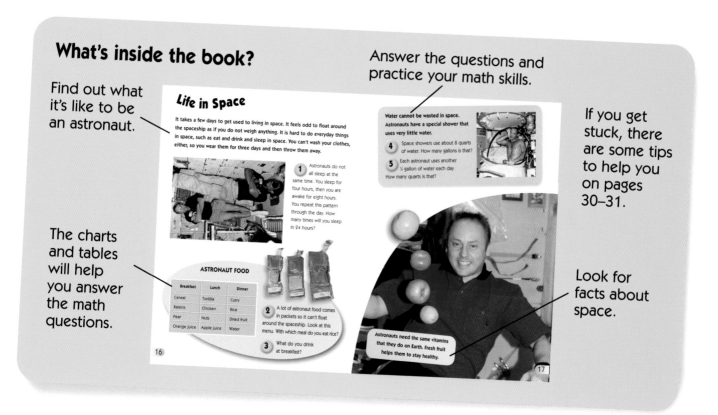

What's inside the book?

Find out what it's like to be an astronaut.

Answer the questions and practice your math skills.

If you get stuck, there are some tips to help you on pages 30–31.

The charts and tables will help you answer the math questions.

Look for facts about space.

Life in Space

It takes a few days to get used to living in space. It feels odd to float around the spaceship as if you do not weigh anything. It is hard to do everyday things in space, such as eat and drink and sleep in space. You can't wash your clothes, either, so you wear them for three days and then throw them away.

1 Astronauts do not all sleep at the same time. You sleep for four hours, then you are awake for eight hours. You repeat this pattern through the day. How many times will you sleep in 24 hours?

ASTRONAUT FOOD

Breakfast	Lunch	Dinner
Cereal	Tortilla	Curry
Raisins	Chicken	Rice
Pear	Nuts	Dried fruit
Orange juice	Apple juice	Water

2 A lot of astronaut food comes in packets so it can't float around the spaceship. Look at this menu. With which meal do you eat rice?

3 What do you drink at breakfast?

16

Water cannot be wasted in space. Astronauts have a special shower that uses very little water.

4 Space showers use about 8 quarts of water. How many gallons is that?

5 Each astronaut uses another ¼ gallon of water each day. How many quarts is that?

Astronauts need the same vitamins that they do on Earth. Fresh fruit helps them to stay healthy.

17

Are you ready to be an astronaut?

You will need paper and a pencil, and don't forget your space suit! Let's go...

Heading for the Moon

You have been chosen to take part in a mission to the Moon. Your rocket will blast off into space and travel 238,855 miles (384317.69 km) to the Moon. Your mission will take about a week. Let's find out about the Moon!

Have you noticed the Moon's changing shape? It takes 29 days from one full Moon to the next. This is called a lunar month.

1 How many days are there in 2 lunar months?

2 Is 29 an odd number or an even number?

THE SHAPE OF THE MOON

The Moon seems to change its shape during the lunar month. Here are some of the shapes we can see.

A   B   C   D   E

3 Which of these shapes is a circle?

4 What is the shape of Moon C?

Moon

Earth

The Moon is about 4 times smaller than Earth.

A journey to the Moon is as far as driving around Earth about ten times! Use the 10x table to answer these questions.

5 Every day you run 3 miles (4.82 km). How many miles would you go if you ran 10 times as far?

6 You love to drink milk. You have 2 cups (0.473 ml). How much would you have if you drank 10 times this amount?

7 You have a pet mouse. Imagine if she were 10 times as long! Would she be the size of:

A a guinea pig   B a dog   C an elephant

Astronaut Training

It takes a long time to learn how to be an astronaut. Your training is hard but fun. You learn how to fly the rocket, how to breathe in your space suit, and how to walk in space. You make friends with the other people training to be astronauts.

ASTRONAUT CHART

Name	Tim	Cilla	Leo
Age	19 years	22 years	25 years
Height	5 feet 9 inches (1.75 m)	4 feet 11 inches (1.49 m)	6 feet 2 inches (1.87 m)

1 You start training with Tim, Cilla, and Leo. It will be ten years before you all go into space. How old will these astronauts be when you go into space?

2 The first rockets ever made were very small. Which of these astronauts would best fit inside a small rocket?

3 Astronauts wear a special suit in space. Space suits weigh around 48 pounds (21.772 kg). 48 comes between 40 and 50. What other whole numbers come between 40 and 50?

FLIGHT TRAINING

As part of your training you have to learn how to fly a jet. It is important for you to be able to steer the plane.

4 The fighter plane below has made a ¼ turn clockwise. Which other planes have made a ¼ turn?

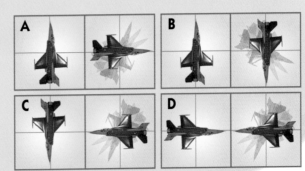

There is no air in space. When astronauts go outside the spaceship, they wear a space suit that supplies them with oxygen.

The Rocket

You have finished your training, and you're ready to go to the Moon. The rocket is ready, too! You go to look at it. It's hard to believe that this will be your home for the next week.

The bottom of the rocket looks like this. It has five pipes. They have been arranged in a pattern like this.

1 Which of these rockets has its pipes arranged in the same way?

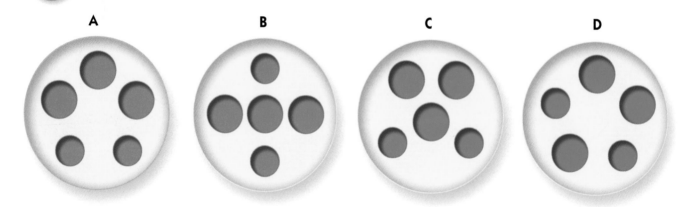

A   B   C   D

2 The rocket can sit on the launchpad for several weeks. This clock shows how many hours, minutes, and seconds there are until its launch. Is this
about a week?   **about 1 day?**
about 2 days?   **about ½ a day?**

Can you find this shape on the tower?

3 How many sides are on this shape?

4 How many corners does this shape have?

The engines are at the bottom of the rocket. The astronauts sit near the top of the rocket.

5 We can find these shapes on the rocket. Can you name them?

Your rocket is ready to blast off into space!

We Have Liftoff!

This is it! You say goodbye to your family and friends and climb into the rocket. You do the final checks and then strap yourself into your seat. The rocket starts to shake. Boom! You have liftoff!

At 10 a.m. the fuel is loaded into the rocket. 3 hours later you get into the rocket. It then takes you 2 hours to do the final checks. 1 hour after that, the rocket launches into space!

1 What time will the rocket be launched?

2 Astronauts have to be good at counting forwards and backwards. See if you can find the missing numbers in these counting patterns.

A   3   6   ?   12

B   25   30   35   ?

C   22   ?   18   16

After liftoff, parts of the spaceship fall away. This makes the spaceship lighter so that it can go faster. This line shows when each part falls off.

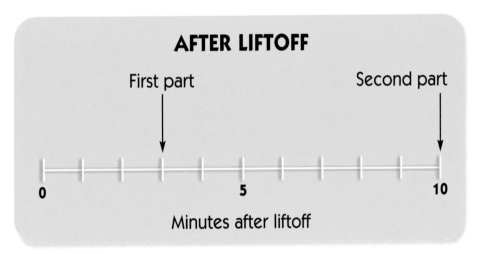

AFTER LIFTOFF

First part   Second part

0   5   10

Minutes after liftoff

3 How many minutes after liftoff does the first part fall away?

4 How many minutes after liftoff does the second part fall away?

Not all of the astronauts on Moon missions actually get to walk on the Moon. For safety reasons, one person has to stay in the spaceship.

The Stars in Space

Your spaceship has a window, and whenever you can, you look out at the stars. Wow! There are so many of them. They seem much brighter in space. A pattern of stars is called a constellation. There are 88 constellations in the sky around you.

Here is a constellation number track.

77		79	80						87	88

1 Which numbers do NOT belong in this number track?

71   85   76   89   86   84

2 This group of stars is called the Plough. How many stars can you see in this constellation?

3 How many lines are there between the stars in the Plough?

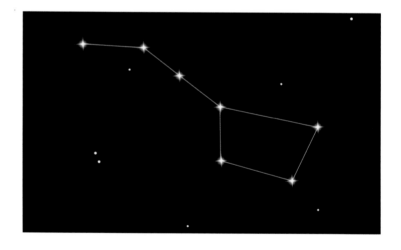

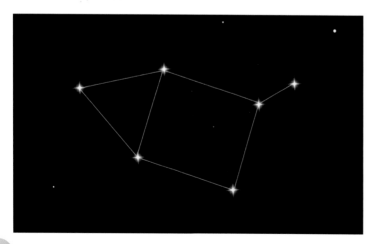

4 You see a new constellation. How many stars make the triangle?

5 How many stars make the rectangle?

There are 7 types of stars. One of the biggest is the red supergiant. It is much bigger than our Sun. A white dwarf is one of the smallest stars. You will have to count stars on your trip. Try this star math.

6 11 red supergiants plus 8 red supergiants

7 14 red supergiants take away 13 red supergiants

8 9 white dwarfs added to 17 white dwarfs

9 30 white dwarfs minus 22 white dwarfs

We can see the stars much better from space. Earth's atmosphere makes it hard to see the night sky clearly.

Life in Space

It takes a few days to get used to living in space. It feels odd to float around the spaceship as if you do not weigh anything. It is hard to do everyday things in space, such as eat and drink and sleep. You can't wash your clothes in space, either, so you wear them for three days and then throw them away.

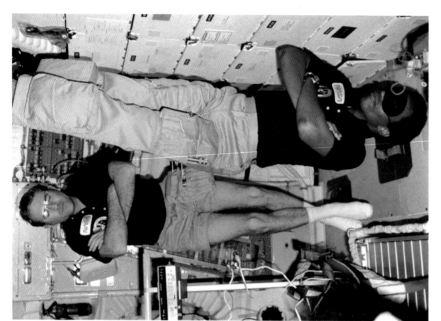

1 Astronauts do not all sleep at the same time. You sleep for four hours, then you are awake for eight hours. You repeat this pattern through the day. How many times will you sleep in 24 hours?

ASTRONAUT FOOD

Breakfast	Lunch	Dinner
Cereal	Tortilla	Curry
Raisins	Chicken	Rice
Pear	Nuts	Dried fruit
Orange juice	Apple juice	Water

2 A lot of astronaut food comes in packets so it can't float around the spaceship. Look at this menu. With which meal do you eat rice?

3 What do you drink at breakfast?

Water cannot be wasted in space. Astronauts have a special shower that uses very little water.

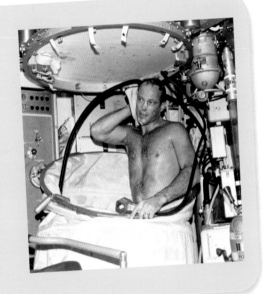

4 Space showers use about 8 quarts of water (7.57 l). How many gallons (liters) is that?

5 Each astronaut uses another ¼ gallon (2.27 l) of water each day. How many quarts (liters) is that?

Astronauts need the same vitamins that they do on Earth. Fresh fruit helps them to stay healthy.

Back at Mission Control

Back on Earth, there are lots of people in the mission control room. They check that the rocket is working properly and the astronauts are healthy. They use computers linked to the rocket to get their data.

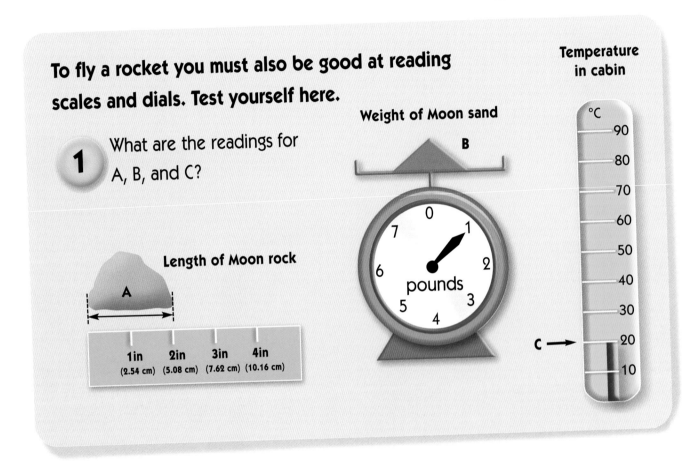

To fly a rocket you must also be good at reading scales and dials. Test yourself here.

1 What are the readings for A, B, and C?

Temperature in cabin

Weight of Moon sand

Length of Moon rock

pounds

°C

1in (2.54 cm) 2in (5.08 cm) 3in (7.62 cm) 4in (10.16 cm)

There are red and green lights on the computers. The green means everything is working, and the red means something is wrong. Look at this pattern of lights.

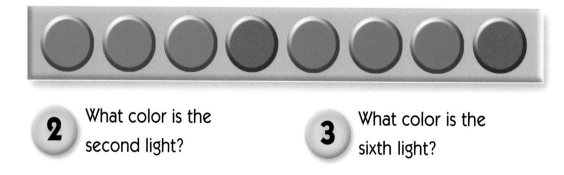

2 What color is the second light?

3 What color is the sixth light?

In space, you and the rest of the crew feel weightless. You can float around the spaceship.

This energy bar feels weightless, too. On Earth it weighs 3 ounces (8.05 g).

4 How much do these bars weigh on Earth?

5 How much do these bars weigh on Earth?

6 Mission control needs to check that you're not too tired and your brain is alert. Here is a thinking puzzle for you. What is the mystery number?

| A mystery number | − | 4 | = | 8 |

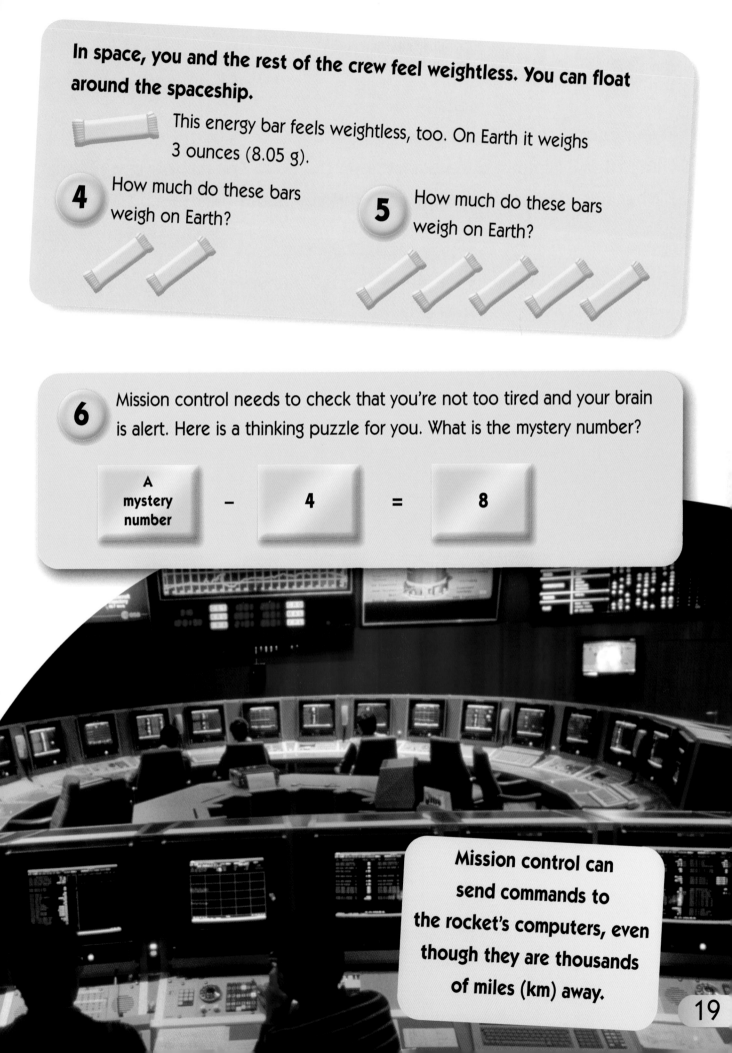

Mission control can send commands to the rocket's computers, even though they are thousands of miles (km) away.

Our Solar System

If your journey to the Moon goes well, you might be chosen to take part in a mission to the planet Mars. Our Solar System has eight planets. Earth is one of them. Astronauts need to know about the other planets.

Look at the picture at the bottom of this page.
It shows all of the planets in our Solar System.

1. Which planets are nearer to the Sun than Earth?

2. Is Mars bigger than Earth?

3. Which is bigger – Earth or Neptune?

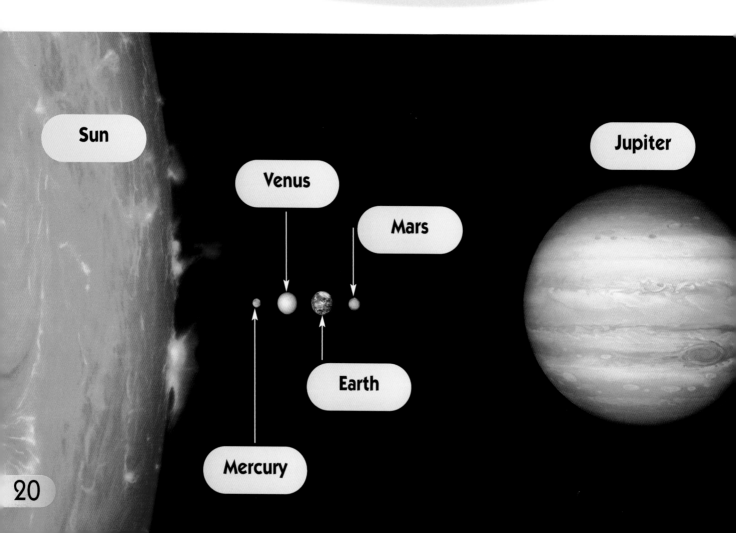

Sun

Jupiter

Venus

Mars

Earth

Mercury

The planets closest to Earth are Venus and Mars.

4 Which of these planets is called the Red Planet?

5 Which of these planets has two moons?

VENUS FACTS
- It is very hot.
- Covered in gases.
- It doesn't have any moons.

MARS FACTS
- It is cold.
- It is called the Red Planet.
- It has 2 moons.

6 Earth has only one moon. Neptune, Jupiter, and Uranus have lots of moons. One of these planets has 15 moons, one has 8 moons, and one has 16 moons.
- Jupiter has the most moons.
- Neptune has the fewest moons.

How many moons does Neptune have? Jupiter? Uranus?

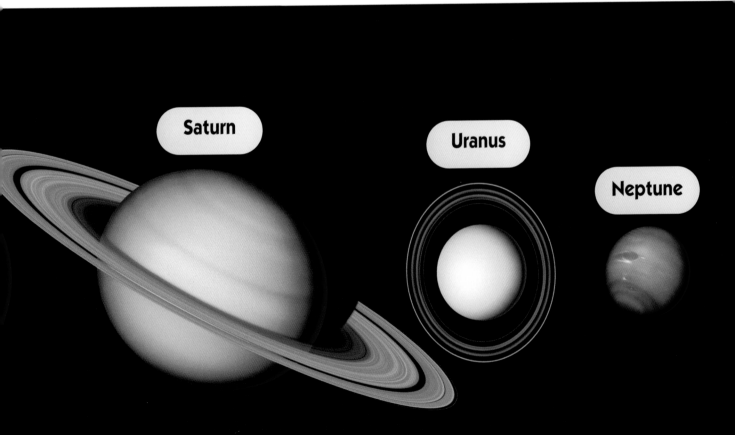

Saturn

Uranus

Neptune

Landing on the Moon

Your rocket is near the Moon. The Moon lander separates from the rocket and takes you to the Moon's surface. You look out of the window. The Moon has rocky mountains and big holes called craters. It is dry and dusty. You and the other astronauts are the only living things on the Moon.

There are big holes, or craters, on the Moon. The craters are made when rocks from space crash into the Moon. Your task is to measure some crater widths. Here are your results:

10 inches (25.4 cm) 1 foot (30.45 cm)
3 feet (91.44 cm) 24 inches (60.96 cm)
½ foot (15.24 cm)

1 Put the measurements in order, starting with the shortest width.

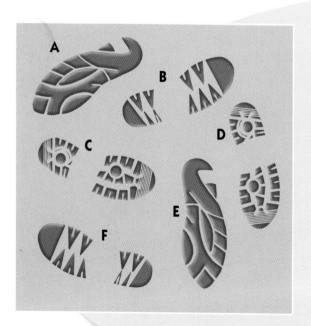

There is no wind on the Moon. You look out of the window and see footprints left behind by other astronauts. Your footprints will also be there long after you leave.

2 Match up the pairs of astronaut footprints.

3 How many astronauts made these footprints?

You won't be the first astronaut on the Moon. The first men to ever walk on the Moon were from the Apollo II, in 1969. Here is their mission calendar:

July 1969					
Sunday		7	14	21	28
Monday	1	8	15	22	29
Tuesday	2	9	16	23	30
Wednesday	3	10	17	24	31
Thursday	4	11	18	25	
Friday	5	12	19	26	
Saturday	6	13	20	27	

July 16 - Blastoff!

July 20 - Landing on the Moon

July 21 - First person steps on the Moon

July 21 - Liftoff!

July 24 - Arrive back on Earth

4 On which day of the week did the the first person step on the Moon?

5 Did the mission take over a week or under a week?

This is it! You're about to step onto the Moon!

Walking on the Moon

The door to your Moon lander opens slowly. You walk down the steps and then step onto the Moon. This is it! You are actually here! Walking on the Moon is fun. You weigh much less here than you do on Earth, and so walking is more like bouncing.

FINDING YOUR WAY

You have a grid map of part of the Moon.

 Moon lander   crater small rock  large rock

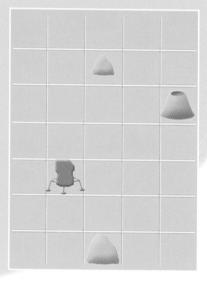

1 The small rock is 1 square right and 3 squares up from the Moon lander. What are the directions from the Moon lander to reach the crater?

2 How would you reach the large rock from the Moon lander?

3 You have been asked to collect some rocks from the Moon. Back on Earth, scientists will study them to find out more about the Moon. You collect 20 pounds (9.71 kg) of Moon rock. How many boxes will you need if each box can carry 4 pounds (1.8 kg) of Moon rock?

4 How many boxes will you need if each box can carry 5 pounds (2.26 kg)?

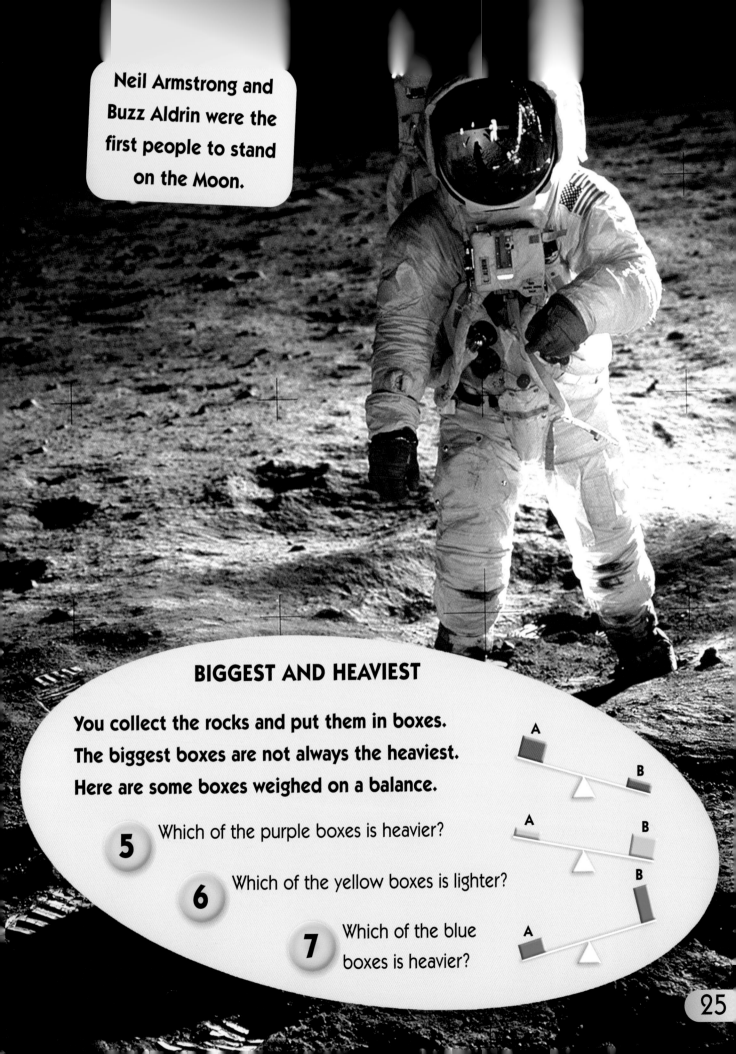

Neil Armstrong and Buzz Aldrin were the first people to stand on the Moon.

BIGGEST AND HEAVIEST

You collect the rocks and put them in boxes. The biggest boxes are not always the heaviest. Here are some boxes weighed on a balance.

5 Which of the purple boxes is heavier?

6 Which of the yellow boxes is lighter?

7 Which of the blue boxes is heavier?

Return to Earth

The rocket is carrying a capsule. When you get near Earth, you all get into the capsule. The capsule comes away from the rocket and brings you back to Earth. You splash down safely into the sea. Your mission has been a success.

The capsule goes very fast.

1 Compare the capsule's speed with the speed of a cheetah and a train. Use this information to put them in order, from the fastest to the slowest.

running cheetah – 60 mph (96.56 kph)
capsule – 24,000 mph (38.624 kph)
fastest train – 250 mph (402.34 kph)

2 The capsule has three parachutes to slow it down. One parachute has 20 strings. What do we need to add to these numbers to make 20?

19   **7**   **3**   **16**

SPLASH DOWN IN THE SEA

You come down into the sea. There are lots of people around, on planes, ships, and helicopters.

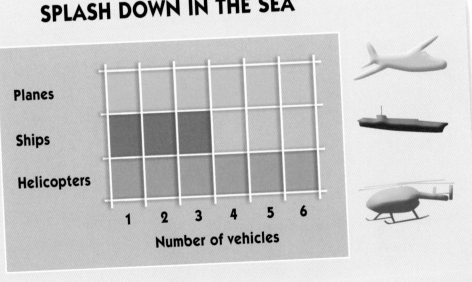

Planes

Ships

Helicopters

1   2   3   4   5   6
Number of vehicles

3 How many helicopters are there?

4 How many vehicles are there in all?

Your capsule splashes into the water. You've made a safe landing.

YOU'RE HOME!

Your capsule lands in the sea at 2:00 p.m. Here are the times that you and the other astronauts actually step out of the capsule.

Leo	2:11 p.m.
Cilla	2:06 p.m.
You	2:13 p.m.
Tim	2:09 p.m.

5 Who is first out of the capsule?

6 How many minutes after landing are all the space team out?

Back Home

You have landed safely back on Earth. It's been an amazing trip. Of course, everybody wants to hear about it. Reporters from newspapers and TV crowd around you, wanting to hear your story. You are famous!

Here's what happens after your capsule crashes into the sea. Do the number puzzles connected to the events. Use the answers to the number puzzles to respond to the questions.

Helicopter ride back to base

1 How many minutes does the helicopter ride take? **Answer:** 8 + the number of days in a week

Clinic for health checks

2 How many doctors examine you? **Answer:** the number of half-inches (centimeters) in 4 inches (10.1 cm)

Talking to the press

3 How many questions are you asked? **Answer:** 2x the number of hours in a day

Family time

4 How many vacation days do you have? **Answer:** the number of nickels in a dollar

5 Each space mission has a badge. This is the Apollo 11 badge. Look at the three badges below. Which badge did your mission choose?

- It has two circles to show Earth and the Moon.
- It has a triangle to represent the rocket.
- It has a square to represent the 4 astronauts on your team. Which is your badge?

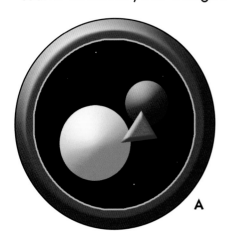

A

B

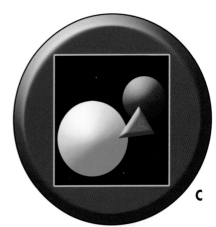

C

The next team of astronauts is ready to go up into space, but your mission is over now.
Well done, astronaut!

Tips and Help

PAGES 6–7

Odds and evens – Even numbers are in the pattern of counting by twos: 2 4 6 8 and so on. Odd numbers are those that are not even: 1 3 5 7 and so on.

PAGES 8–9

Adding ten – When you add ten to a number, you need only increase the tens in that number by one ten; so 19 has one ten (and nine ones) and if we add a ten to make two tens, the answer is 29 (two tens and nine ones).

A ¼ turn – There are four quarter-turns in one complete turn.

Clockwise – Clockwise is the direction in which the hands of a clock move.

clockwise

PAGES 10–11

Number of hours in a day – There are 12 hours in half a day, 24 hours in one day, 48 hours in two days, and 168 hours in a week.

Shapes – Remember these shapes:

Cylinder: the two faces at the ends of a cylinder are circles.
Cone: a cone has a flat, circular base.

PAGES 12–13

Telling time – The little hand points to the hour. To find out when the rocket will be launched, move the little hand 3 hours, then 2 hours, and then 1 hour.

Number track – The number track here is measuring minutes. Each mark in the track means one minute.

PAGES 14–15

Adding up – The words "plus," "add up," "add to," and "sum" all mean the same. You can add numbers in any order. Here's a tip for solving addition problems with 9. In your mind, change the 9 to 10. Add the numbers and then take away 1 from the answer. Example: 9 + 17 is the same as 10 + 17 – 1. Use the same idea for problems with 11. Change the 11 to 10.

Taking away – "Take away," "minus," and "subtract" all mean the same.

PAGES 16–17

Day – There are 24 hours in a day; that is, from midnight to the next midnight.

PAGES 18–19

Scales and dials – In math these help us measure. Check which unit is shown. For example, this scale shows us pounds.

Counting by twos – Count aloud: 2 4 6 8 10 12 14 16 18 20. It is useful to remember this pattern.

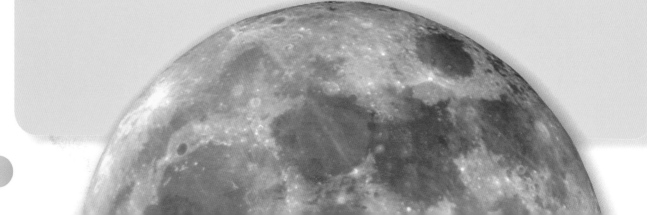

PAGES 20–21

Comparing things – We say "bigger than" when we compare two things, and "biggest" when we compare three or more than three things. We say "more" or "fewer" when we compare two numbers and "most" or "fewest" when we compare three or more than three numbers.

PAGES 22–23

Putting measures in order – Check that all the measurements are in the same unit, that is, are they all inches or feet (centimeters or meters)?
If not, change them all to the same units. Next, put the numbers in order. The smallest whole numbers have no tens (only ones or units). They are the numbers 1 2 3 4 5 6 7 8 9. Next, look for numbers with only 1 ten and put the number with fewest ones first, then the others. Then see if there are numbers with more than 1 ten and put those in order according to the number of tens they have, and so on.

Calendar – On this calendar, reading down tells us the dates for a week. Reading across tells us the dates for a particular day (for example, all the Sundays).

PAGES 26–27

Making 20 – It is useful to know the pairs of numbers that add up to 20. See if you can continue the pattern:
0 + 20
1 + 19
2 + 18……

Bar graph – This graph compares two kinds of information. This bar graph compares numbers of kinds of vehicles. One unit in the graph means one vehicle.

Digital time – We can tell digital time by reading the hours and then the minutes. For example, 8:27 a.m. means the time is 27 minutes past 8 in the morning.

PAGES 28–29

Measures – Remember there are:
• 7 days in a week
• 2 halves in a whole
• 100 cents in a dollar.

PAGES 24–25

Grid maps – You can work out the routes on a grid map by moving right or left and up or down (or up or down and then right or left).

Sharing – When we break up an amount or a number into equal parts, each part is a share or fraction of the whole. This is called sharing or dividing.

Answers

PAGES 6–7

1 58
2 odd
3 E
4 semicircle
5 30 miles (48.28 km)
6 20 cups (4.7 l), or 10 pints (5.6 l)
7 a dog

PAGES 8–9

1 Tim – 29 years old
   Cilla – 32 years old
   Leo – 35 years old
2 Cilla
3 41, 42, 43, 44, 45, 46, 47, and 49
4 A and C

PAGES 10–11

1 D
2 about 1 day
3 4
4 4
5 cylinder and cone

PAGES 12–13

1 4 p.m.
2 A is 9, B is 40, and C is 20
3 3 minutes
4 10 minutes

PAGES 14–15

1 71, 76, and 89
2 7
3 7
4 3
5 4
6 19 red supergiants
7 1 red supergiant
8 26 white dwarfs
9 8 white dwarfs

PAGES 16–17

1 2
2 dinner
3 orange juice
4 2 gallons (7.57 l)
5 1 quart (.943 l)

PAGES 18–19

1 A is 2 inches (5.1 cm), B is 1 pound (.45 kg), and C is 20°C
2 green
3 green
4 6 ounces (170 g)
5 15 ounces (425.2 g)
6 12

PAGES 20–21

1 Mercury and Venus
2 no
3 Neptune
4 Mars
5 Mars
6 Jupiter has 16 moons, Uranus has 15 moons, and Neptune has 8 moons

PAGES 22–23

1 ½ foot (15.2 cm), 10 inches (25.4 cm), 1 foot (30.4 cm), 24 inches, (61 cm) 3 feet (91.4 cm)
2 A and E, B and F, C and D
3 3 astronauts
4 Sunday
5 Over a week

PAGES 24–25

1 3 squares right and 2 squares up
2 1 square right, 2 squares down
3 5 boxes
4 4 boxes
5 B
6 A
7 A

PAGES 26–27

1 capsule, fastest train, running cheetah
2 1, 13, 17, and 4
3 6 helicopters
4 14 vehicles
5 Cilla
6 13 minutes

PAGES 28–29

1 15 minutes
2 8 doctors
3 48 questions
4 20 days
5 C